Elephant Dance

A Journey to India

For Till, Vanessa, Nicola and Hartmut with love — T. H.

For Jake — S. M.

Barefoot Books
124 Walcot Street
Bath
BA1 5BG

This book was typeset in Veljovic
The illustrations were prepared in acrylic

Graphic design by Katie Pringle
Colour separation by Grafiscan
Printed and bound in Hong Kong by South China Printing Co. Ltd

This book has been printed on 100% acid-free paper

ISBN 1-84148-916-6

British Cataloguing-in-Publication Data:
a catalogue record for this book
is available from the British Library.

1 3 5 7 9 8 6 4 2

Elephant Dance

A Journey to India

written by **Theresa Heine**

illustrated by **Sheila Moxley**

Barefoot Books
Celebrating Art and Story

When Grandfather came from India it was cold.
Anjali knitted him a red woolly scarf
and Ravi bought fleecy slippers for his feet.
'Is it hot in India, Grandfather?' asked Ravi.

'Yes indeed, Ravi,' said Grandfather.
'The sun is a most fierce fellow,
hotter than a hundred cooking fires.
At dawn he rolls into the sky like a fiery ball,
then he uncurls and he is a ferocious tiger!

For dinner he eats red chillies.
He is so very hot and thirsty
he growls and roars all day.
In the evening, when the stars
begin to shine along the Milky Way,
he drinks a bowl of coconut milk,
and then he falls asleep.'

Grandfather brought presents for everyone:
A blue sari for Mum,
a sandalwood box for Dad,
silver bangles for Anjali
and a red and gold kite for Ravi.

Grandfather and Ravi took the kite to the park.
'Grandfather,' said Ravi, 'what is the wind like in India?'

'When she blows from the western desert lands, Ravi,
she is strong. Like a wild horse, she stamps and snorts.
She snatches the children's kites and storms away with them,
beyond the hills and over the ocean.

'Sometimes the wind is a gentle one.
Then she pit-pats through the trees,
hushing the leaves to sleep.'

'And what is the rain like?' asked Ravi, as they sheltered
under the trees.

'The monsoon rain is like a curtain, silver like Anjali's bangles.

It cascades like a waterfall from the sky,

making many mirrors on the ground.

Raindrops scurry to and fro like little silver fish.

When the sun and rain meet

they make a rainbow,

s - t - r - e - t - c - h - i - n - g

over the sky.'

'Is it the same as the rainbows
I see here?' said Ravi.
'A rainbow in India, Ravi beta,
is seven silk saris hung across the sky to dry;
red as the watermelon,
orange as lentils,
yellow as saffron,
green as the parakeet,
blue as the kingfisher,

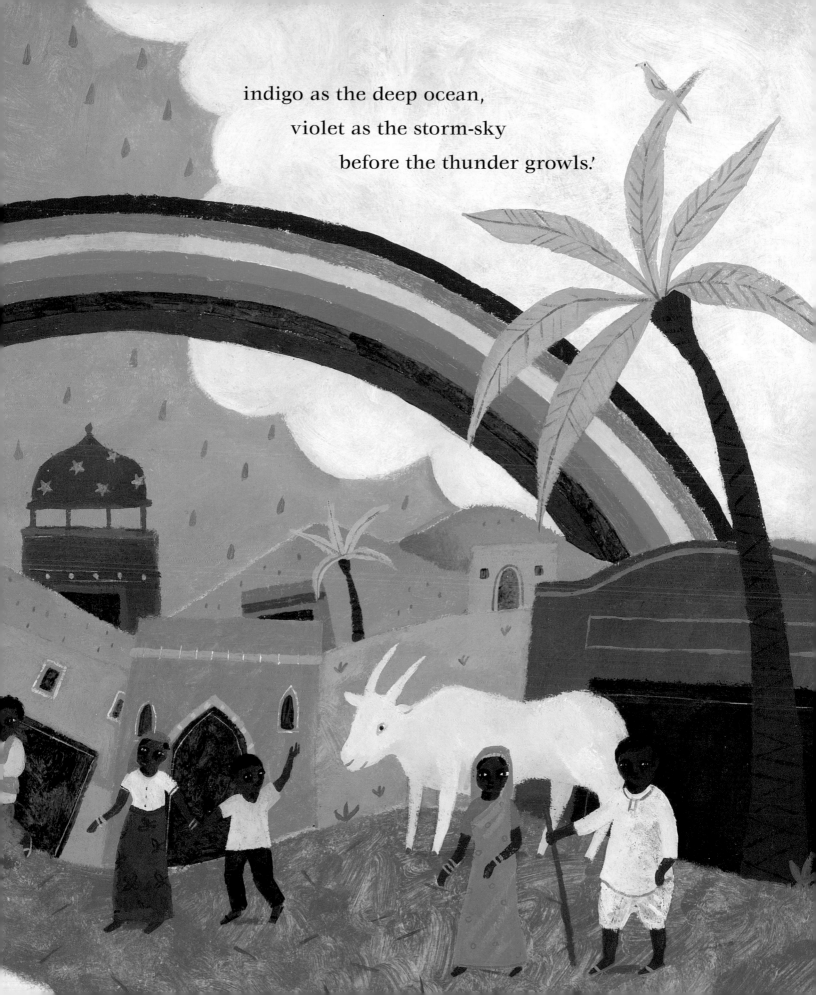

indigo as the deep ocean,
  violet as the storm-sky
    before the thunder growls.'

Ravi took Grandfather shopping in the market.
They bought ghee and ginger,
fish and lentils,

yoghurt and cucumber,
and a bamboo flute for Ravi.

'Is there snow in India, Grandfather?' said Ravi.

'Yes, Ravi. High in the north are the Himalayan mountains.

The snow on their tops is a giant ice cream,

very cold and white,

melting on your tongue.

It keeps the mountain tops cool

when the tiger sun roars at midday.'

It was supper-time and soon the kitchen was full of delicious smells.

Mum and Anjali cooked daal in a pan with cloves and cardamom.

They fried the fish and onion in ghee until they were golden.

Dad ground turmeric, coriander and cumin,

and mixed them with the fish and the yoghurt.

Anjali fetched the rice and Ravi set the table.
Then they sat down to eat.

'Grandfather,' said Ravi, 'are you very old?'

'Hush now, Ravi,' said Mum.

But Grandfather laughed. 'Yes, Ravi beta. As you see
I am old and brown like garden soil,

and wrinkled as a walnut.

My teeth are not many and I cannot chew so well,

but I manage with what I have.'

'Have you ever seen an elephant, Grandfather?' said Anjali.
'Indeed I have,' said Grandfather.
'When I was a child like you and Ravi,
I saw elephants walk in a procession on the feast of Divaali.
They wore silk howdahs, blue as the royal peacock.
Princes rode on their backs.

The hot streets teemed with people,
and everywhere were flowers;
garlands of sweet jasmine and morning glory,
hibiscus blossoms, cream and red and yellow,
which we tucked behind our ears.
We ate sticky sweets of coconut and almonds
and lit fireworks in the street.
We heard the chimes of bells and gongs,
the beating of many drums.'

Ravi took out his flute and blew into it.
'This is my elephant dance, Grandfather.'

Grandfather smiled. 'That is a most fine
elephant dance.
You must practise very much and maybe one day
an elephant will dance for you.'

PAKISTAN

TIBET

NEPAL

THE RIVER GANGES

ARABIAN SEA

INDIA

INDIAN OCEAN

After supper Anjali got out her paints and pens, and she and Ravi
and Grandfather drew a map.

'The shape of India,' said Grandfather, 'is the ear of an elephant.'

They drew in tigers and peacocks and crocodiles,
elephants, snakes and monkeys.

They coloured in the great river Ganges
and the ice cream peaks of the
Himalayas.

They painted the western deserts,
the elephant forests of the east,
and the great tiger sun of
the south.

BHUTAN

ANGLA-
DESH

MYANMAR
(formerly BURMA)

BAY OF
BENGAL

NORTH

WEST

EAST

SOUTH

GULF OF
THAILAND

'Grandfather,' said Ravi, as he got ready for bed.

'Do you love me?'

Grandfather put his arms round Ravi. 'Ravi beta,

you are as warm as a newborn kid,

as soft as the frangipani blossom,

as sweet as the juice of the mango.

And I love you very much.

Now it is time for sleeping.'

Ravi slept and dreamed of a deep green forest
where moonlight fell in a silver stream.
In the night grass a great grey shape swayed its head
and moved its large feet.

Ravi raised his flute to his lips
and as he played
he saw the elephant
dancing a silent dance.

Ravi's Elephant Dance

Living in India

Geography

India is in South Asia, and covers most of the Indian subcontinent. The land and sea area combined make it the sixth-largest country in the world, with a population of over a billion people.

There are three major seasons in India, and they differ from region to region. The coldest weather lasts from December to February. From March until May it is very dry and hot. The monsoon rains come in June, bringing long, heavy spells of hot, humid rain. The monsoon moves south during the summer months of June until September.

The Himalayas are a series of mountain ranges, stretching across India, Nepal, Bhutan and Tibet. The highest mountains in the world are in the Himalayas: Mount Everest, Mount K2 and Mount Kanchenjunga.

India is home to some of the largest rivers in the world, including the sacred rivers Ganges, Yamuna and Saraswati. The River Ganges is mentioned in holy Hindu texts and holds great religious significance. Babies are frequently baptised in its waters and adults come to drink and bathe. The Saraswati river is now dry, but was considered a powerful river in ancient times.

India is one of the leading producers of wheat, cotton and rice. Wheat is a staple ingredient in North Indian cuisine, while rice is important in South and East Indian dishes. India's major cities are New Delhi, its capital city and political centre, Bombay, Calcutta and Chennai.

Religion and Culture

The family in this story is Hindu. Hinduism is the main religion in India, and centres around the belief that there is one universal God, who takes the form of many different gods, both male and female. Most Hindu families revere the three gods of the Hindu trinity, or Trimurti, who are Brahma, the Creator, Vishnu, the Preserver, and Shiva, the Destroyer. Hindus worship these gods using statues, which they bathe in milk and decorate with flowers during prayer rituals. Other religions practised in India include Sikhism, Buddhism, Islam, Christianity, Zoroastrianism and Judaism.

There are many festivals in the Hindu religion, which are calculated according to the lunar calendar, rather than the solar one. They are often celebrated with an explosion of colour and joy. Elaborate meals and delicious sweets are prepared, with family and friends coming together to share in these festivities.

One of the most important Hindu festivals is Divaali, the Festival of Lights. During Divaali, Hindu families light oil lamps in their homes in honour of Lakshmi, Goddess of Wealth. They also celebrate the return of Prince Rama, hero of the Indian epic, *The Ramayana*, to his home Ayodhya after a long exile and victory over Ravana, the Demon King.

India's national flower is the lotus. This vibrant flower only grows in shallow waters, with the leaves and petals floating above the surface.

India is a country of rich cultural heritage, and the proud home of the Taj Mahal, one of the Seven Wonders of the World. This beautiful tomb was built during the Moghul empire, by its fifth Emperor Shah Jahan, in loving memory of his queen Empress Mumtaz Mahal. It took twenty-two years to complete and has become one of the most famous images in the world.

The Animals of India

Indian Elephant

The Indian elephant has been a symbol of India for centuries. It is smaller than the African elephant and is easy to tame. It is very intelligent and has an amazing sense of balance. In the hot sun, it uses its big ears as fans, flapping them to keep cool, while it sucks up water through its long trunk to use as a shower hose. Indian elephants are vegetarians and eat lots of plants and fruits, but they have a special liking for sweet treats such as mangoes, coconuts and sugar cane!

In the past, when the country was divided into many small kingdoms, Indian elephants were used to carry members of the royal families. They have also been used in forestry and to this day, they continue to help humans to protect forests from poachers. They can also be found in temple precincts and are still ridden in processions at important festivals and weddings. The 'howdah' which is mentioned in this story refers to the large box-like seat which people sit in for these processions.

Bengal Tiger

There are more wild tigers in India than in any other part of the world. They are known as Bengal or Indian tigers. There are far fewer of them now than a hundred years ago, as poachers hunt them for their fur and organs.

The orange fur and vivid black stripes of tigers make patterns that are unique

to each one, like human fingerprints. Unlike other large cats, tigers love water and are very good swimmers.

Indian Cobra

The Indian cobra is a large, poisonous snake which spits jets of venom when it is attacked. It is an important creature in Hindu culture, with the Festival of Serpents (Nagapanchami) being held in August. For this occasion, wild cobras are brought into villages to be fed, and small statues of the snake are displayed for worship.

Indian Peacock

The peacock is India's national bird, and it is thought to be sacred because it is the carrier of the Hindu god Karttikeya. It is one of the largest flying birds in the world and is most famous for its beautiful train of bright blue, golden and green feathers. Only the male peacock has this grand train, which it displays to the female to attract her.

Hanuman Langur

Hanuman langurs are a variety of monkey. They are revered across India as the descendants of the Hindu monkey god, Hanuman. Hanuman langurs are found all over India, from the mountains and forests of the Himalayas to the busy cities of the south. Many Hanuman langurs live near Hindu temples, where they are well fed by visitors. They are also accomplished thieves!

Food and Spices

India is famously known as 'the land of spices', because of its wide array of fragrant blends and seasonings. Here are a few staples of Indian cookery:

Daal

Daal is a term used to refer to all pulses, like lentils, kidney beans and chickpeas. These pulses are used to make a stew-like dish, also called 'daal', which is flavoured with spices. Daal can be cooked with a variety of different pulses and is often served as an accompaniment to the main meal.

Clarified Butter (Ghee)

Ghee is a semi-liquid form of butter, in which the milk solids and water have been removed through heating and straining. It is often used as a substitute for oil in cooking and is a staple ingredient for the preparation of both sweet and savoury Indian dishes.

Saffron (Kesar)

Saffron, the world's most expensive spice, comes in threads, which come from a small purple flower, the *Crocus Sativus*. It adds a bright yellow colour to food and has a very strong, distinctive taste. It is used in small amounts in many sweet and savoury Indian dishes, and is considered a symbol of hospitality.

Turmeric (Haldi)

This mustard yellow spice looks very similar to saffron and is often added to curries. It is thought to be lucky and is used in prayer rituals (pooja) and at weddings, when women apply it to their hands and face.

Red Chillies (Lal Mirchi)

Chillies taste as hot as they look! Red chillies add flavour and heat to popular Indian dishes like curry and daal.

Ginger (Aadrak)

Ginger is a root with a slightly peppery bite. It is a very aromatic spice which, as well as being included in savoury dishes, is often added to Indian teas to help prevent colds and flu. It is also the main ingredient in snacks and drinks like gingerbread and ginger ale.

Mango (Umbri)

The mango is called the 'King of Fruits' in India. This bright yellow fruit has delicious, sweet flesh which is often used in *kulfi*, an Indian ice-cream flavoured with saffron, almonds and milk.

Barefoot Books
Celebrating Art and Story

At Barefoot Books, we celebrate art and story with books that open the hearts and minds of children from all walks of life, inspiring them to read deeper, search further, and explore their own creative gifts. Taking our inspiration from many different cultures, we focus on themes that encourage independence of spirit, enthusiasm for learning, and acceptance of other traditions. Thoughtfully prepared by writers, artists and storytellers from all over the world, our products combine the best of the present with the best of the past to educate our children as the caretakers of tomorrow.

www.barefootbooks.com